Original title:
Climbing the Canopy

Copyright © 2025 Creative Arts Management OÜ
All rights reserved.

Author: Rosalie Bradford
ISBN HARDBACK: 978-1-80566-779-7
ISBN PAPERBACK: 978-1-80566-799-5

Notes from the Skyward Boughs

Up in a tree, I made my stand,
With squirrels debating, and birds so grand.
An acorn fell, right on my head,
"You should wear a helmet!" the raccoon said.

My buddy the owl gave a strange hoot,
"Watch out for branches, don't lose your boot!"
I slipped and twirled, did an acrobatic dance,
The frogs cheered me on, I took my chance.

A twig snapped loud; I thought I must fall,
But landed right next to a reviewing mall.
The chipmunks all laughed, ran off with my snack,
"What's better than nuts? A friend's heavy pack!"

The view from the top, I must admit,
Is worth every tumble, every misfit.
With laughter aloft, we share our cheer,
As nature's own circus rings in my ear.

The Whispered Path Above the Earth

Up in the heights, where the critters play,
I trip on a vine, oh what a display!
The leaves rustle gently, they seem to tease,
"Can you dance like us?" swayed by the breeze.

I spotted a slug, he wobbled right by,
"Slow and steady," he said, with a sigh.
He dared me to race, but all I could do,
Was laugh as I tumbled, that slippery goo.

An owl winked down, perched high and proud,
"You're quite the performer! Come join the crowd!"
With squirrels as judges, I took my bow,
While the robins all chirped, and the sun took a vow.

So up in the branches, where giggles abound,
In a world made of laughter, joy can be found.
With friends by my side, we'll share every chase,
A silly parade, in this leafy embrace.

Serenade of the Upper Leaves

Up above, where squirrels dance,
A chubby raccoon takes a chance.
He swings on branches, noisy show,
While down below, ants plot a foe.

In leafy caverns, secrets hide,
A wise old owl counts them with pride.
"Whooo's that moving?" he hoots so loud,
While the leaping frogs croak, feeling proud.

Finding Solace in the Treetops

A parrot laughs from high above,
Sipping nectar, a sweet love.
He teases branches with a tease,
While bumblebees buzz with ease.

In treetop realms, the giraffe sighs,
Wearing a crown of twinkling eyes.
He tries to fit in with the crew,
But, oh dear, he's too tall for the view!

A Quest for Canopy Dreams

An adventurous monkey swings high,
Looking for dreams beyond the sky.
"Grab that vine!" his buddies yell,
As laughter echoes – oh so well!

The tree frogs join with a bold croak,
Telling tales of an ancient oak.
They hop from leaf to shimmering leaf,
Sharing stories of joy and grief.

Enchanted by the Woodland Sky

Above the ground, where magic thrives,
A party holds, and everyone jives.
Raccoons bring snacks; they dance in glee,
While owls spin tales of what they see.

A slow sloth joins, with a lazy grin,
"Will someone help me? I can't begin!"
They chuckle loud, as laughter swells,
In this forest, all is well.

Reaching for the Blushing Sky

I swung my legs, a daring feat,
Reaching up high, oh what a treat!
My hat flew off, with such a flair,
Hoping the birds won't start to stare.

With branches low and vines that twist,
I climbed so high, I crossed my wrist!
A squirrel smirked, his cheeks so fat,
I told him, "Buddy, where's your hat?"

The Green Balcony's Embrace

Up on the leaves, I take a stand,
Pretending I'm in a rock band!
The ants below, they start to sway,
I'll need a mic, or at least a tray.

A frog croaked loud, a wild encore,
As I danced on vines, the branches bore.
"Careful," they whispered, "don't lose your grip!"
But I just twirled, I'm on a trip!

Breathing with the Whispering Branches

Winds start to chuckle, a ticklish breeze,
As leaves conspire, plotting with ease.
I laugh, I shout, the trees reply,
"Let's play tag, come on, oh my!"

A branch caught my foot, a tangled mess,
"Hey! Mind your manners, you're such a pest!"
With roots that giggle, I sway and bend,
My leafy pals turned into friends.

Shadows Beneath the Canopy

In the shadows, I found a prank,
My shadow danced, a merry plank.
I tripped on roots, the ground did squeak,
The trees just chuckled, feeling meek.

With every stumble, a new twisted tale,
My shadow grinned, adding to my wail.
"Ouch!" I exclaimed, but laughed instead,
Who knew the ground could be so wed?

Treetop Aspirations

In the upper limbs where squirrels meet,
I dreamed of heights, my heart a beat.
Instead of trailing roots below,
I jumped for joy and waved hello.

But branches creaked and twigs went snap,
I swung too wide, fell in a lap.
The birds just laughed, they thought it grand,
As I flopped down like a dog so bland.

Echoes of the Breeze-Embraced

The wind whispered secrets through the leaves,
I listened close, amidst the eaves.
"Don't trip on vines, and mind the bees!"
But I just laughed, as I caught a sneeze.

With bright ideas floating up high,
I gathered courage, a tree-bound spy.
Yet somehow tangled up in my shirt,
I dangled there, much to my hurt.

Flight of the Woven Branches

I strapped on wings made of sticks and dreams,
Hoping to soar, or maybe just gleam.
But gravity chuckled, pulling me down,
Becoming the jester, a tree-bound clown.

I tried to glide but tripped on a groove,
Among the branches, I made my move.
Yet laughter erupted from every side,
As I bounced from a branch, my pride took a ride.

Nature's Airborne Mosaic

A patchwork quilt of green and blue,
I thought I'd soar, but what a view!
From wobbly branches to roots so deep,
I pictured my triumph, then fell in a heap.

With blossoms tangled in my hair,
I laughed at the clouds, unaware of despair.
"Just a tree hugger," I grinned in delight,
As owls rolled their eyes in the fading light.

In the Arms of Ancient Giants

High above, the branches sway,
Where squirrels plot their grand ballet.
With acorns tossed like tiny grenades,
One almost landed—what a charade!

The leaves whisper secrets vast and grand,
While birds get tangled in their own band.
I dance with shadows, twirl and spin,
While nature chuckles at my silly grin.

Tryst with the Woodland Heights

Branches stretch to tickle the sky,
I wave at a raccoon passing by.
"Hello there!" I shout with glee,
He just stares; he must not see me!

Swinging from vines like a wild fool,
I trip and fall; oh, what a duel!
The moss below offers a soft embrace,
While tree trunks laugh at my clumsy grace.

Touching the Spirit of the Forest

Up in the boughs, I spot a nest,
The baby birds hold an open fest.
Pecking and poking, they sing their song,
While I try to join, but I'm all wrong!

A woodpecker joins with a tap-tap beat,
I nod my head to his rhythmic tweet.
But tripping on roots, I lose my step,
And tumble down—oh, what a misrep!

A Walk Among High Horizons

The sunlight dances on emerald leaves,
As I slip on a twig; oh, how it cleaves!
With every step, a symphony plays,
Of rustling flora in amusing arrays.

A butterfly flutters with flamboyant flair,
I try to catch it, but it just won't care.
Instead, I land in a patch of dirt,
And laugh at my outfit—what a quirky shirt!

Heartbeat of the Verdant Roof

In green pajamas, squirrels jump,
They think they own this leafy clump.
Raccoons in hoods, look quite refined,
With acorn hats, their fashion's blind.

A parrot laughs, 'You call this fun?'
While ants march by, 'We're number one!'
The branches sway, a wobbly dance,
Nature's circus, take a chance!

With every leap, a twig will break,
A squirrel sighs, 'Oh, for heaven's sake!'
The chattering birds, just toss a jest,
In this wild realm, we're all a mess.

But laughter echoes, fills the air,
As leaves catch whispers, tales to share.
In this wild world, where chaos reigns,
We find our joy, through all the pains.

View from the Treetop Edge

The world below seems far away,
From up on high, we shout and play.
With branches stretched like limbs so wide,
Swinging from side to side, we glide.

A bumblebee buzzed, 'What's the deal?'
He's unimpressed by our high-steel.
The ground, so dull, lacks our style,
While up here, we can laugh awhile.

A breeze blows through, a ticklish tease,
It swirls around like playful bees.
The view is grand, if you don't fall,
Just keep it steady; hear the call!

So join the fun, do not delay,
Let's build a world where we can play.
Above the ground, the sky's our friend,
At this height, the laughter won't end.

Nestled in Nature's Cradle

Up high within the tangled trees,
We swing and sway with playful ease.
The branches hold our silly crew,
And promise, no one will fall through.

Beneath us roll the rhymes of life,
Down there, they struggle in their strife.
We laugh aloud, a merry band,
While poking fun at all that land.

A leaf falls down, it lands just right,
A silly hat for a bird in flight.
Oh, what a style, so fresh, so bold,
Nature's fashion show, behold!

So settle in, this is the place,
Where giggles dance and smiles embrace.
In nature's lap, we find our cheer,
Nestled here, let's spread some cheer!

Twilight in the Leafy Summit

As twilight paints the sky with flair,
We gather 'round without a care.
The fireflies make a dazzling show,
While crickets chirp fast and slow.

The sun bids adieu, the stars awake,
A squirrel slips, but makes no break.
He twirls around, as if to say,
'Let's party on; it's night, hooray!'

Witty owls have wise things to share,
'You're too loud, but we don't care!'
With laughter echoing through the leaves,
We spin our tales, as night weaves.

So raise a cheer for evening's fun,
In this high space, we're not yet done.
For under stars, we dream and play,
In the summit's arms, we'll sway away.

Heightened Dreams Above

In a world so high, we tiptoe with glee,
A squirrel in shades, giving eye-winks for free.
We dance on the leaves, in a floral parade,
While bees wear bow ties, in suits they've made.

Ants sport top hats, on their leafy stage,
Acorns gossip softly, sharing their age.
With laughter that drapes through branches so wide,
We twirl in the breezes, on nature's joyride.

Ladders of Light and Shadow

Ropes of sunshine dangled, as we played hide and seek,
With shadows that giggled, oh what a mystique!
A parrot in a tutu twirled on a perch,
While the owls wore glasses for a scholarly search.

Frogs in formation, they leap and they croon,
Singing their anthems beneath the round moon.
New vines stretch their limbs as if waving hello,
While critters in bow ties all put on a show!

The Secret Life Above Ground

Whispers of laughter bubble through the leaves,
With mushrooms in slippers sharing their eves.
A raccoon with a monocle scans for his snack,
As chipmunks have meetings, planning their attack.

Fireflies act sassy, they flash and they glide,
While branches whisper secrets that they cannot hide.
A squirrel in a cape zips past with a cheer,
In this high-flying world, there's nothing to fear!

Echoes from the Upper Boughs

From twigs that are ticklish to petals that sing,
The canopy chuckles, embracing the spring.
A gathering of butterflies, making a mess,
As they flit and they flutter in colorful dress.

Breezes tell stories of critters so bold,
As they tickle the branches with laughter untold.
The sunbeams play tag in a game of delight,
In this roof of the world, oh what a sight!

The Infinite Above

In the jungle's lofty realm,
Lemurs swing with flair and glee,
Dancing on the branches' helm,
While squirrels plan their latest spree.

Parrots gossip, green and bright,
With tales of nuts and mango treats,
As monkeys hold their acorn fight,
And plan to drop them on your feet.

The vines talk back, they're full of sass,
Each twist and curl a jest in tune,
A sloth declares, 'I'll make it fast!'
But naps have claimed him 'neath the moon.

Up above, the sunlight beams,
Through leafy curtains, shining wide,
While laughter echoes, bouncing dreams,
In this green circus, joy can't hide.

Whispers of the Treetops

In canopies of leafy green,
Squirrels plot their nutty schemes,
While chattering birds humbly preen,
And hatch the wildest of their dreams.

A sloth, so slow, departs anew,
To raid a berry bush delight,
But every time he turns, who knew,
A hungry vine could cause a fright!

The breezes tickle branch and bough,
As laughter dances with the leaves,
Each whisper brings a playful vow,
To join in on their merry eves.

Above the ground, in vibrant play,
There's nonsense wrapped in every curl,
With every laugh, the skies turn gray,
And turn the forest into swirls.

Ascending Through Verdant Veils

With climbing shoes made of bamboo,
A toucan's laugh rings through the trees,
He shows me how to soar and view,
A world that's buzzing with such ease.

Each branch becomes a very stage,
Where antics roll like tumbleweed,
While monkeys mime in playful rage,
And juggle fruits at high speed.

The ferns are giggling, swaying low,
As butterflies flirt, flit, and zip,
And every breeze, a riddle's glow,
In nature's whims, we take a trip.

Up here, the ground seems far away,
With every leap, we start to cheer,
In this green circus, we must stay,
As laughter rings from ear to ear.

The Heights Above the Forest Floor

In leafy heights, I trip and sway,
With branches playing follow-there,
A toucan shouts, 'Hey, it's okay!'
As I perform my best despair.

The squirrels cheer, and leaves applaud,
As I fumble through this jungle art,
A quick salute, a graceful nod,
Then fall right back—oh, what a start!

With monkeys grinning all around,
They toss me snacks from up on high,
It's kind of funny, I've found,
Just floating by with a sigh.

Above the ground, the laughter soars,
In this green gym where we all play,
With every plummet, joy explores,
The heights above keep troubles at bay.

Clusters of Life Above

Up in the trees, where the squirrels play,
A raccoon shimmies, but fears the day.
Bees wear tiny hats, buzzing with pride,
While chubby old owls just roll in the tide.

Monkeys throw fruit, what a messy feast,
As sloths chill out, the kings of the least.
Funky little frogs croak in delight,
Joking with snakes who sleep through the night.

Parrots gossip, with feathers all bright,
While chattering critters take off in flight.
Life's a parade in this leafy bazaar,
Where laughter works wonders, and dreams go far.

Where the Sky Meets the Leaves

Atop the branches, the view is grand,
With chipmunks debating who's king of the land.
A bear on a branch, what a sight to see,
Waving to tourists – 'Come visit me!'

The wind does a dance through the leafy green,
Whispering secrets of sights unseen.
Treetop high-fives from a wise old crow,
Clapping his wings, putting on quite a show.

A raccoon's lost hat falls down from a height,
And the squirrels all giggle, what a funny sight!
Tales weave through branches, from dusk until dawn,
Where the sky meets the leaves, all worries are gone.

Secrets in the Branching Spiral

In the tangle of limbs, the gossip flows,
A toad sings tales of the sun and the snows.
With a twitch of a tail, the antics begin,
As wily old foxes argue to win.

Curly vines twist in a playful embrace,
While mushrooms wear caps at a top-secret place.
Rabbits in boots run from shadows up high,
Flopping around, as the owls watch them fly.

The whispers of leaves share a ticklish tease,
Of acorns that fall with the greatest of ease.
What mischief awaits in this forested maze?
Where secrets unfold and the critters all graze.

Soaring Spirits of the Forest Grove

Up in the treetops, where giggles abound,
The spirits of laughter are always around.
Squirrels in capes jump from branch to branch,
While badgers perform an impromptu dance.

The breeze carries stories of daring delight,
As butterflies twirl in a colorful flight.
Chipmunks are jesters in nature's grand play,
Throwing acorns for fun, just to brighten the day.

In this merry grove, every critter's a star,
From the tiniest ant to the big-tailed spar.
Soaring high spirits and joy all aglow,
In the vibrant expanse of the forest below.

Towards the Celestial Canopy

Up we go, like squirrels with flair,
Hopping branches without a care.
Swinging low, then soaring high,
Hoping we don't wave goodbye!

Leaves like umbrellas, green and wide,
We're secret agents, let's not hide.
Peeking at nests, oh what a show,
Is that a baby? No, just a toe!

Dodging spiders with webs so great,
They're not for us, we can't be late!
One last jump, a tumble and roll,
Did I just shuffle? Oh, bless my soul!

But with laughter echoing through the trees,
We find delight in every breeze.
Nature's playground, not a care at hand,
In our tree-top town, we make our stand!

A Path Among the Maple Fronds

In vibrant leaves, our path we trace,
Like curious mice, we step with grace.
What's that sound? A branch like a drum,
Or just my buddy? Oh, here they come!

What's that up there? A chubby bird,
He thinks he's grand, haven't you heard?
He struts and squawks, a feathery king,
Hello, fine sir, can you even sing?

Watch your step, there's sticky sap,
It pulls you in with a gooey clap.
I'm stuck! Oh no! What a silly plight,
Just take the plunge; it could be quite a bite!

So on we venture through shade and light,
Embracing the quirks, what a grand sight!
Maples wave as if saying, "Stay!",
In our leafy kingdom, let's dance and play!

Venturing into the Lush Above

Off we go, into leafy heights,
Armed with snacks and hopes so bright.
With every twig, we hear a crack,
Hope it's a bonus, not a wooden whack!

Look! That branch looks like a slide,
Let's take a ride, let's not abide!
A jolly yelp as we zoom down,
Whee! Look at us, kings of this crown!

A rustle, a wiggle, what could it be?
Oh, it's just a leaf dancing free.
But now there's mud, and oh what fun,
Splats everywhere, our journey's just begun!

With giggles echoing through the air,
We dance like monkeys without a care.
In this green thrill, we feel alive,
Among the vines, we thrive and thrive!

The Rise to Verdant Horizons

Upward we bounce, a vibrant cheer,
Through tangled vines, nothing to fear.
A swing like Tarzan, but less of the grace,
Flailing limbs, a hilarious race!

Oh, behold! A caterpillar parade,
They scoff at our jumps, how unafraid!
"Join us," they say, "with a feathered hat!",
"Oh dear," we giggle, "where's our acrobat?"

Branches above, ripe fruits galore,
Challenge accepted! A fruit ninja's score.
But slipping banana? Grapes like bullets?
Oh no! We're dodging like the best of mullets!

With laughter our guide, we scale with glee,
In this green world, carefree as can be.
So let's embrace all quirky sights,
In our hilarious climb to dizzy heights!

Journeys Through the Verdant Vault

In leafy realms where critters play,
I lost my shoe—what a day!
A squirrel sighed, then stole my snack,
While I just stood, too shocked to act.

The vines conspired, oh what a tease,
They wrapped my legs, I swayed with ease.
A parrot laughed, it knew my plight,
And joined my dance, what a silly sight!

I found a branch that swung like mad,
It flung me wide—just like a fad!
I twirled around, arms flapping free,
My friends all gasped, "Is this a spree?"

But then I stumbled, oh what a fall,
Landed right near the tree trunk tall.
Laughter echoed from high above,
Turns out the branches all have love!

Skyward Spirits

Up in the leaves where giggles thrive,
A raccoon joined, oh how we jive!
We wore our hats, mismatched in style,
The trees all clapped, they liked our guile.

The branches swayed to a tune so bright,
I tripped and tumbled, what a sight!
A monkey swung on a vine nearby,
Charmed by my moves, he gave a cry.

The breeze was warm, a tickle on skin,
I danced with shadows, let the fun begin!
But a gust so strong sent me for a spin,
I grasped a twig—now where've I been?

As I dangled there in a windmill twist,
I spotted a sloth, could not resist!
"Help me down!" I called, feeling quite daft,
He just gave me a smile, then started to laugh!

The Treetop Symphony

In the treetops we made a band,
With acorns as drums, oh wasn't it grand!
An owl played flute, a crow on the mic,
As the branches swayed to our wild hike.

The sunlight winked, shadows danced in tune,
A beetle grooved beneath the moon.
We strummed on vines, our laughter loud,
As squirrels gathered, forming a crowd.

The melody soared through the leafy maze,
While birds dropped in for a concert craze.
A chameleon changed colors, a sight to behold,
"Don't steal my spotlight!" I playfully scold.

But just then, a gust swept us away,
Our stage collapsed, oh what a display!
We landed safely, giggling in heaps,
Nature's laughter, a joy that never sleeps.

A Tapestry of Branches

A tapestry woven with giggles and glee,
Each branch a story, come climb with me!
I twirled around, caught in a mess,
With vines as my dress, oh what a guess!

A slinky squirrel made quite a show,
Taught me to hop, gave me the lowdown flow.
A parrot squawked, "You've got some flair!"
As I fell right back, head first in midair!

The leaves all rustled, their whispers a cheer,
"Don't worry, dear friend, we're all gathered here!"
With every tumble, my giggles went high,
The branches below whispered, "You'll fly, oh my!"

So up I went, not a worry in sight,
With every misstep, pure delight.
Together we danced, as day turned to dusk,
Under the stars, in laughter, we trust!

Explorations Beyond Earth's Grasp

Up I go with a squeak and a wiggle,
Hoping not to trip on a branch or a sprig.
The birds all chirp as I step on their toes,
This tree is alive with giggles and blows.

Twirling like a squirrel with nothing to lose,
I dodged a few bees in their terrible snooze.
If I tumble down, at least I'll have tales,
Of face-plants in moss, and fondness in gales.

Fingers stretch high to catch leafy delight,
With laughter erupting, I dance in the light.
A twig snaps, oh dear! What a clumsy affair,
But up here, with nature, nothing can compare.

So onward I bounce with joy in my heart,
This green, leafy realm is a whimsical art.
Who knew that the branches would giggle and sway?
Adventure awaits in the best kind of way!

Revelations Among the Branches

I spotted a bird with a curious grin,
As I clambered up, my adventure begins.
He tweets a tune, as if to declare,
"Hey, you down there? How's the ground? Try the air!"

With each higher step, I feel quite like Tarzan,
I swing on a vine like a nutty young man.
The view gets absurd - a pirate's delight,
I swear I can see the whole world from this height.

But wait, what is that? A nest filled with snacks!
The birds look at me with their judgmental backs.
My stomach grumbles loud, I laugh with a grin,
Who knew this ascent would bring me such sin?

So up to the top, where the goofballs reside,
I'll join in the laughter and let loose my pride.
With each branch I conquer, I'm feeling quite spry,
Guess what? I think trees make the best places to fly!

Embracing Heights in Nature's Splendor

I tiptoe through leaves that rustle and shake,
Beneath mighty branches, my plans start to bake.
A raccoon gives me a once-over glance,
And I wonder if critters also love to dance.

A swing here, a hop there, who knows where I'll land?
The squirrels all chuckle; they've got it all planned.
With each bounce upward, my giggles ignite,
The trees cheer me on, such a comedic sight!

My hat takes a dive, it sails off like a kite,
The squirrels are laughing, it's quite quite a sight.
But with every mishap, I learn how to cope,
These moments enhance both my laughter and hope.

Finally perched high, I spread out my arms,
The world's little secrets, its magical charms.
A crown of green foliage sits snug on my head,
With joy in my heart, and a knapsack of bread!

The Journey to the Tree Top

I set off this morning, my mission in play,
To scale up the woods and be silly today.
With each step I take, I can hear a loud cheer,
The creatures are rooting for me - oh dear!

Down below, the ants plot their tiny parade,
While I'm kicking up leaves like I'm in a charade.
Branches are tickling my shoes as I glide,
What's that? A frog joins my wild, goofy ride!

The higher I go, the funnier it seems,
A squirrel chases me, am I living in dreams?
He squeaks and he darts, with me he does race,
I'll call him my friend in this nutty embrace!

At last, I arrive at the top of my climb,
And shout out loud, "This is truly sublime!"
With the wind in my fur and a smile that gleams,
I'll forever cherish these tree-top daydreams!

Skylines of the Forest's Poetry

In trees so tall, we play peek-a-boo,
With squirrels who wear hats, to win the view.
They chatter and squeak in a curious tone,
While I wonder if they'd rather stay home.

A toucan juggles nuts, what a sight!
While I try to balance, oh, what a fright!
Laughter erupts like a burst of spring,
As birds serenade us, it's a whimsical fling.

Branches sway subtly, like they are dance,
While I bust my moves, in a fancy pants.
They giggle and sway, calling me ludicrous,
But I'm sure these trees are quite used to us!

So up we go, through the green and brown,
Each step a giggle, no hint of a frown.
In this jovial jungle, we leap and we twirl,
Adventure awaits, in this leafy swirl.

Harmonies Above the Ground

Amidst the leaves, we hear a tune,
A frog on a branch sings to the moon.
His voice, quite deep, makes the ants conspire,
To form a chorus that climbs higher and higher.

A monkey swings by, with a pie in hand,
Yelling, "Who's hungry? I made it on demand!"
But as he slips, oh what a sight,
A pie in the air, a true aerial flight!

Parrots chat gossip about a lost sock,
While I hang upside down—oh, what a shock!
Everyone's laughing, it's a raucous affair,
As feathers and giggles fill up the air.

So here we celebrate, those harmonies strong,
With laughter and melodies, we'll sing along.
In this playful habitat, we dance on high,
As the forest's spirits wave us goodbye.

Ascensus of the Canopy

With a vine for a rope, I start my ascent,
Hollering out, 'I'm a pirate, not spent!'
But the branches all snicker, with leaves all aglow,
'We've seen better pirates, just thought you should know!'

A raccoon in a bowtie gives me a cheer,
While I try not to slip, oh dear, oh dear!
He's got quite the pose, looking debonair,
While I'm arms and legs tangled, without a care.

Each vine I grasp is a giggle galore,
As I trip and I tumble, then holler 'Encore!'
The trees are my audience, the critters my fans,
With each little blunder, they conjure their plans.

So up I go, in this green comedy,
Waving to bumblebees, "Come laugh with me!"
Amidst this madcap, I find joy anew,
Who knew that tree limbs could talk smack too?

Rhythms in the Arched Branches

Wobbling like jelly, I'm painting the sky,
With branches like trampolines, oh my, oh my!
A woodpecker nods, says, "Can you keep pace?"
As I bounce off the leaves in this dizzying race.

The owl looks down, trying not to smirk,
"Is that a dancer, or a peculiar quirk?"
But the cicadas hum, their music quite loud,
Supporting my moves, they're a buzzing crowd!

On the way to the top, there's a dizzying spin,
As I twirl with the lizards, we're all wearing grins.
They cheer as I stumble, a ballet in trees,
While dragonflies join with a flurry of ease.

So join the frolic, in these arched branches wide,
Every giggle and tumble, I'll take in stride.
With laughter and rhythm, we'll soar through the green,
In this festival of fun, I'm the star of the scene!

Unveiling the Leafy Overhead

Up among the branches high,
A squirrel sneezes, oh my!
He thinks he's caught a bug or two,
But it's just my shoe, oh boo!

A parrot laughs, on a bough,
"Why are you here?" Oh, tell me how!
I say, to see the world anew,
He squawks, "Try asking the view!"

A raccoon peeks from leafy shade,
With clever eyes that will not fade.
"Got any snacks?" he quickly grins,
"Just nuts," I reply, "but there's bins!"

As I frolic through the green,
Life above is quite the scene.
A dance begins, with leaves afloat,
I trip and spin, what a funny coat!

Treasures Hidden in the Upper Woodland

Look up high, what do I see?
A pizza slice? Oh, that can't be!
But there it is, my lunch in flight,
A hungry bird, what a delight!

Nestled deep in a crooked tree,
A treasure chest filled with glee.
But when I peek inside the cracks,
It's just old socks and some snacks!

"Got a map?" a chipmunk squeaks,
With tiny paws, he nervously tweaks.
He points to branches, tall and wide,
"X marks the spot, let's take a ride!"

As I follow his tiny lead,
I stumble over roots, oh dear speed!
The real treasure is laughter loud,
In this woodland, I'm quite proud!

Touching the Pulse of the Green Canopy

Up above where the sunlight plays,
A frog croaks out a tune that sways.
"Do you have rhythm?" he asks with flair,
I dance around, quite unaware!

A monkey swings with grace profound,
"Catch me if you can!" he bounds around.
But my foot slips on a branchy song,
And I tumble down, where I belong!

With each thump upon the dirt,
The woodland chuckles; I can't assert.
A worm wriggles, "Hey, are you fine?"
I laugh and shout, "Just a little wine!"

The trees sway gently in the breeze,
Watching my antics with teasing ease.
In the pulse of greens around, I shout,
"Who knew this place could make me pout?"

Opening to the Forest's Invitation

The forest calls, with a giggle so neat,
"Come take a look at our leafy street!"
I stroll through ferns, they wave with glee,
"Join the party, won't you agree?"

With butterflies flitting, all dressed to impress,
One lands on my head, what a funny mess!
"Oh, nice hat!" a squirrel does tease,
I bow with laughter, "Can I take these leaves?"

A deer appears, with a wink and a nod,
"Let's dance together, it's not very odd."
But as we jig, I trip on my lace,
And laugh as I tumble, oh what a race!

Among the trees, I feel so free,
Their whispers of fun surround me with glee.
In this wild ball, I find what's true,
Nature's a comedian, full of goo!

Whispered Hues of the Canopy

A squirrel in shades of blue,
Steals my sandwich, what to do?
Leaves giggle as they sway to tell,
That nature's pranks fun as a spell.

Where branches tickle the sky so wide,
A toucan sports a funky stride.
With colors that pop like confetti's dash,
I laugh as I tumble, I hope I don't crash.

Amidst the leaves that whisper low,
A raccoon joins in the show.
He juggles acorns with such flair,
I clap my hands, a woodland affair!

In this bright world of green and cheer,
Nature's jesters, come draw near.
With every flinch and playful swoop,
Life's a circus, join the troop!

Lifting Above the Understory

Bamboo shoots that dance in line,
Look at me, I'm feeling fine!
Slipping past in a leafy waltz,
Who knew trees could have such faults?

A parrot quips, "Who's got the flair?"
As monkeys swing without a care.
They knock my hat off with a swoosh,
I shout, "Be gentle, it's no moosh!"

In my mind, I'm a jungle star,
But I trip over roots, oh so bizarre!
With every step, I squeak and squawk,
While vines giggle and trees mock.

Yet up I go, despite the clatter,
Who knew nature had such a chatter?
Amidst the giggles, I make my pledge,
To be the king of the leafy hedge!

Embracing the Open Sky

Bouncing high on a branch so sly,
I yell to the clouds, "Oh my, oh my!"
Birds fly by with a wink and roost,
While I flail about like a funny goose.

Up above, the view is grand,
But my balance? Not so planned!
I slide down leaves with a comedic flair,
Spinning like a top in midair.

A raccoon chuckles, "What's that you've got?"
"Just a funny fall—did I give it a shot?"
As I scrape my knees from the tumble and roll,
The trees laugh softly, "You've got soul!"

But with each bump, I rise and sing,
The laughter here is my favourite thing.
In the heights where the breezes play,
I dance like a fool—who needs ballet?

Fleeting Glimpses of the Upper Realm

Up here in the branches high,
I spy a lizard, oh my, oh my!
In polka dots, he strikes a pose,
As giggles bubble from my toes.

A sloth drags by, oh what a sight,
Moves slower than a traffic light.
I can't rush; he'll take his time,
While I break into a silly rhyme.

With every flap and clumsy twirl,
I'm crowned the jester in this whirl.
A squirrel shakes nuts with a wink,
"Join the fun! What do you think?"

So I leap and I bound with laughter bright,
Tickling the leaves in sheer delight.
With every giggle and silly cheer,
I dance with the branches, no doubt, my dear!

Ascendant Serenade

Up the branches, I see squirrels dance,
Their nutty antics, they take a chance.
With every step, I scrape my knee,
Who knew tree limbs could threaten me?

The leaves above me whisper low,
"You're not a bird; you sure can't flow!"
I grin back with a silly shout,
In this green world, I'm full of clout!

A Canopy of Stars

Searching for a place to sit,
I find a branch that seems legit.
But when I plop, it gives a crack,
I hope the tree won't take me back!

The stars peek through like winking eyes,
While critters gossip, sharing lies.
Is that a rabbit up a pine?
Or just a raccoon, sipping wine?

The Breath of the Tall Ones

The forest breathes, it sniffs and blows,
With every sway, it surely knows.
A chubby bear gives me a nod,
I think I just made a forest god!

And up above, I hear a cheer,
From birds who think I have no fear.
I wave and slip, a graceless fall,
Next time, I'll just take the mall.

Twilight Among Treetops

As twilight sneaks in, I start to sway,
Did I just hear a tree say, "Hey!"
A breeze goes by, it teases my hat,
I'm dodging branches like a combatant!

The night is young, with laughter bright,
As owls hoot jokes in the pale moonlight.
I shrug and flop on leafy beds,
Tomorrow, I'll stay close to my threads.

Interwoven with the Sky

Up high with squirrels, what a sight,
I wave to the birds, oh what a flight!
Swinging on branches, never a care,
Laughing as I tumble, up into the air.

My shoe's on a branch, lost in the green,
While the raccoons giggle, they're quite the scene!
Tickling the leaves, they shake in delight,
Who knew such heights could be a comic plight?

With tree trunks as ladders, I reach for the top,
Where bees throw a party, and all the critters hop!
I'm king of the jungle, or so I proclaim,
While ants start a mutiny, what a wild game!

Finally perched safe, what a view to share,
The world looks so silly from way up in the air!
I'll toast with acorns, oh what a spree,
As the wind tells secrets, just my tree and me.

Embracing the Above

Balancing on branches, I dance with glee,
While a parrot squawks, 'Come join the spree!'
With each silly stumble, I giggle and fall,
For every great stumble, I'm having a ball!

Up in the treetop, a pineapple grows,
Though I'm just a kid, no one really knows!
Inventing great games with twigs and with leaves,
While ants take my snacks, oh how they thieve!

In my leafy castle, I rule with flair,
A crown made of flowers, I don't have a care!
Each branch like a stage, for my one-person show,
While the squirrels are critics, 'a five-star encore!'

Oh, what a funny life up here in the blue,
With laughter and antics that never feel through!
So here's to the high life, where fun never ends,
With tree-top adventures and giggling friends!

Shadows and Silhouettes among Limbs

In the shade of the branches, shadows play,
I'm skipping and tripping, hip-hip-hooray!
With the light shining through, it's a dance in the air,
As the leaves clap along, without a single care.

A raccoon pops out, says, 'What's all this noise?'
With a wink and a giggle, he joins in with poise!
Together we sway like the wind-whispered tree,
Creating our own little forest jubilee.

Monkeys nearby, in their circus attire,
Swinging and flipping, oh they never tire!
I'm a tiny acrobat, trying hard to impress,
While the owls just stare, in their wise way, no less.

Each bend of the branch brings a new little laugh,
With ants playing tag, oh what a daft path!
As shadows grow long, I'm still lost in cheer,
In this forest of fun, without a single fear.

Where Roots Meet the Clouds

When roots tickle toes, it's all out of whack,
I'm weaving through grasses, can't find my snack!
With giggles and wiggles, I bounce like a kite,
Hoping that sunshine will guide me to light.

I trip over gnomes and jump over frogs,
While a lizard zooms by, in a blur of bright snogs!
The sunbeam peeks down, with a wink so sly,
Inviting us up, to bask in the sky.

Among all the roots, I hear whispers of fun,
As the earth grins wide, and says, 'Let's all run!'
So I take to the branches, with friends by my side,
In this wacky tree world, I'll always confide.

As clouds drift and dance, right above my head,
I giggle with glee and float where I tread!
In a place full of whimsy, I finally see,
That fun never stops in my own leafy spree!

In Search of Aerial Light

Up high in branches, I wave my hands,
Trying to touch down the sun's warm bands.
With squirrels laughing, they tease my quest,
While I tumble and roll, in jest I jest.

Bouncing on trunks, like a pogo stick,
In my head, I'm mighty—quite the big trick!
But gravity pulls with a funny might,
As I crash in the leaves, what a silly sight!

Pine cones raining down, like nature's confetti,
I blend in with twigs, feeling quite petty.
Caught in a tangle, I hardly care,
For sunbeam selfies, I'm ready to share!

Swinging from vines like a playful monkey,
Excited to find where the sun feels funky.
In pursuit of laughter, up, down, I weave,
In this goofy forest, I never believe!

Stories Told by Rustling Leaves

The rustling leaves tell tales of old,
Of naughty raccoons and secrets they hold.
Whispering softly, with chuckles and grins,
Life's an adventure, let the laughter begin.

A bird with a crown, thinks he's quite grand,
Preening and posing, he strikes a stand.
But a gust hits him, and what a surprise!
He flips and he flops, right before our eyes!

Branches giggle as they sway to and fro,
While the wind plays tag in a leafy show.
I gather the stories, one by one shared,
With trees as my witnesses, never a care.

Every creak and crack, is a chuckle anew,
As nature performs in a wild, silly view.
So I sit with my snacks, beneath the green dome,
Listening and laughing, my heart feels like home.

A Symphony of the Elevated Green

A chirp, a rustle, the orchestra's play,
While I dance on the branches, in a whimsical sway.
The leaves start to clap, in rhythm they cheer,
As squirrels join in, bringing snacks to share!

A cacophony of barks, and an owl's delight,
They sing out their tunes from morning to night.
With each little tumble, a giggle escapes,
Nature's humor wraps us in leafy capes.

The sunlight beams through, like a spotlight on me,
I twirl 'round the trunk, feeling fancy and free.
Frog in the bog joins with a ribbiting beat,
While I bust out my moves, oh, isn't life sweet?

Stepping lightly like shadows, we dance on the floor,
Tree tops our stage, we're forever encore.
In this wild little concert, we're all in on the fun,
With nature's loud laughter, 'til the day is done!

Where Birds Sing in Elevated Sanctuaries

High above the ground, the birds take flight,
With melodies ringing, oh what a sight!
A feathered choir in a sunlit spree,
Their notes float down, just like confetti.

The chattiness flows, with gossip they share,
While I eavesdrop quietly, without a care.
"A worm is too squishy!" one little chick beams,
"Let's dive bomb the cat! It's better than dreams!"

With splashes of color, they dart to and fro,
While I hold my stomach, bursting with woe.
For my mission is clear, to join in their song,
But my voice comes out sounding all kinds of wrong!

So here in the branches, I laugh with my crew,
The trees sway with joy, and they dance too.
In this haven of giggles, we all find our place,
Living high in the humor, where smiles interlace.

Skylight amidst the Foliage

A squirrel flashed by, oh what a sight,
He stole my sandwich, took off in flight.
I chased him 'round, but soon lost track,
I guess I'll find lunch where the leaves are stacked.

With branches like arms, they wave and sway,
I dodged a branch, ne'er thought I'd play.
Nature's a prankster, it seems so true,
I laughed at my fate in this leafy zoo.

Secrets in the Upper Realm

I heard a rustle, was it a bird?
Or just my imagination, how absurd!
A pair of raccoons looked down with pride,
"Come join our party, come take a ride!"

They brought out snacks, oh what a feast!
But all they had was a leaf-wrapped yeast!
I grinned and nibbled, quite out of place,
In this high-up world, with a bushy face.

The View from the Arboreal Edge

Perched on a limb, I'm king of the trees,
But the wind's got jokes, it's got me on my knees.
I tried to strike a pose, but then went whoosh,
The branches giggled, what a silly swoosh!

I spotted a view, oh what a tease,
The neighboring tree was flaunting its leaves.
"Look over here," they'd sway and shout,
I waved back, thinking, "I'll figure this out!"

Canopy Drifter's Song

I drift like a leaf, in a breeze so grand,
Dancing with shadows, oh isn't it planned?
The birds sing a tune that's quite out of sync,
I joined in their chorus, not stopping to think.

A branch gave a creak, a wink from above,
It told me, "Just sway, don't fall for love!"
The squirrels let out a giggly cheer,
As I tripped on a vine, oh dear, oh dear!

Whispers of the Treetops

The squirrels chatter, oh so loud,
In their acorn suits, they feel so proud.
A branchy dance, they leap with glee,
And shout, "Look at me! I'm a monkey's plea!"

The raccoons giggle, plotting their scheme,
Stealing snacks like it's a wild dream.
They tumble down, a furry parade,
Complaining about the games they played.

The wobbly owl hoots a silly tune,
With notes so off, they make squirrels swoon.
"Come join my band!" it oddly requests,
Yet all the birds just laugh with zest.

The breeze carries laughter, such sweet delight,
As leaves rustle softly in the fading light.
The treetops are vibrant, a playful scene,
Where every creature reigns as queen or king!

Reaching for the Sunlight

Tall vines tease the clouds above,
"Hey there, sunshine! We're ready to shove!"
With playful twirls, they stretch and sway,
While mocking shadows, they giggle and play.

A parrot squawks with a wink and a nod,
"Can we borrow your glow, oh great, sunny god?"
It strikes a pose, all feathers and flair,
Then tumbles down, with a half-hearted air.

A gecko's grip is quite the sight,
As it slips and slides, oh what a fright!
"Gravity jokes? Not funny, I swear!"
Then falls with a splat, and the leaves declare.

Yet up they go, these characters bold,
In their airy kingdom, both silly and gold.
With giggles and grins, they dance in the light,
What a wild world, full of pure delight!

Ascending Green Horizons

A sloth in shades, moves way too slow,
"Why rush?" it asks, as the world below.
"Life's a lazy climb, with snacks along the way,
Just chill up here, we'll live all day!"

The monkeys swing, with jumps from a branch,
"Bet you can't keep up, let's take a chance!"
With playful shrieks, they leap in delight,
As the sloth just grins, too cozy to fight.

The flowers giggle in the playful breeze,
"Why not dance with us, oh we're such tease!"
The leaves start to swirl in a merry ballet,
While the sun shines down, saying "Who wants to play?"

With each tiny step, they find their groove,
From feathery ferns to the bugs that move.
Life's little quirks, all woven in cheer,
In green horizons, laughter rings clear!

A Dance Among the Leaves

In a leafy waltz, the branches sway,
"Come join our party, don't be cliché!"
The bumblebees buzz, in sync with the breeze,
As they float and dip with such graceful ease.

A chipmunk hops, in a fancy tux,
As it twirls around, sharing little clucks.
"Watch my moves!" it shouts with flair,
Then stumbles and lands, but hey, don't despair!

The wind hums a tune, ever so sweet,
Tickling the leaves, with a rhythmic beat.
Dancing with shadows, a whimsical ride,
Every tree joins in, even the ones that hide!

In this wooden disco, they all come alive,
With laughter and joy, spirits thrive.
So twirl and leap, in every direction,
For life among the leaves needs no correction!

Stride into the Emerald Air

With each step up, I giggle loud,
As branches wave, they're quite the crowd.
The squirrels laugh, they tease my hair,
I'm not quite sure who's more aware.

Leaves rustle secrets, whispers float,
A raccoon glances, then starts to gloat.
I trip on roots, but still I scheme,
To conquer heights, or so I dream.

Birds chirp loudly, dapper in ties,
They laugh at me, a clumsy rise.
But here I am, still on my quest,
To prove that I can be the best!

With every slip and every slip-up,
I drink nature's coffee from a big old cup.
The clouds above, they cheer me on,
As I laugh and play 'til the break of dawn.

Dance of the Canopied Breeze

The wind takes me on a joyful spree,
Twisting and turning, just like me.
As I prance through the leafy maze,
I dance with shadows in sunny rays.

A parrot squawks, it calls my name,
Wings like rainbows, oh what a game!
I flap my arms, a silly sight,
Trying to soar, taking off in flight.

A butterfly winks, then flits away,
While I tumble down, what can I say?
Laughter echoes in this lofty space,
As I land on a pile of soft green lace.

The laughter of trees is music sweet,
They sway and spin to my ungraceful beat.
And though I'm not sure I'm fit for the prize,
At least I'm winning at laughing skies!

The Poetry of Heights Unseen

In the realm of heights, I search for rhymes,
With every step, I trip on climes.
The boughs above, they beckon me,
To write my verses among the trees.

A quirky owl gives a knowing hoot,
As I dance with vines, what a cute pursuit!
How do I find the right kind of line,
When gravity's laughing and keen to malign?

Branches become my rickety stage,
With critters clapping in pure delight and rage.
I stumble again, oh what a sight,
But poetry's born in this wonderful plight.

Each misplaced footstep, a stanza unfolds,
In this whimsical world, where laughter molds.
So here's to the fun, so wild and free,
Where every misstep's a line in my spree.

Nestled in the Cottonwood Crown

Perched high up, I see the whole scene,
A funny sight, like a living cartoon screen.
With branches like arms, they wave me near,
While giggling squirrels throw acorns in cheer.

The breeze whispers jokes, I can't catch them all,
As I tumble and tumble, then trip and fall.
With feathered friends laughing, what a parade,
In the heart of the wood, I'm never afraid.

Every mishap is simply a giggle,
As I wiggle and jiggle, oh what a riddle!
The trees form a circle, a jovial crowd,
For a performer such as me, oh so loud.

So here I shall dance in this leafy delight,
With acorn applause and sunlight so bright.
Nestled snugly, I conjure up dreams,
Of reigning supreme in my forested schemes.

Between Earth and Sky's Embrace

Up high, the branches sway and shake,
Squirrels gossip, causing a ruckus and quake,
A parrot in shades of neon blabber,
Laughing at the clumsy human labor.

Swinging on vines, a mishap's in view,
A dance with gravity, just hope I don't spew,
Fruits scatter like confetti from my grip,
And the birds cheer me on, a raucous trip.

With every misstep, I chuckle in glee,
The ground's far away, oh look at me!
Caught in a net of green, what a sight,
In the fuzzy web of nature's delight.

A leaf slices air like a banana peel,
Down I go, what a hilarious deal!
With a tumble I land, grinning wide,
Amongst branches and laughter, I'll abide.

The Green Bridge to Heaven

A vine stretches out, a bridge of fun,
To cross over joy, where worries are none,
A monkey giggles, with mischief and flair,
As I wobble and teeter, lightly on air.

Leaves whisper secrets, a rustle and tease,
I trip on a twig, oh no, not the bees!
A butterfly laughs, doing loop-de-loops,
While I stumble in rhythm with nature's troops.

Corny jokes echo from the bushes around,
As critters compete for the silliest sound,
Lost in the laughter, I bounce and sway,
Swinging from branches, I'm finding my way.

A squirrel juggles nuts, what a quirky show,
Just one little slip, and oh no—down I go!
From the green bridge, I tumble and roll,
But laughter is the treasure, and that's my goal.

Echoes of a Leafy Realm

In a leafy realm, where the giggles abound,
The echoes of laughter can always be found,
A crow cracks a joke, oh what a wise bird,
But I laugh so loud, I'm sure it's absurd.

Through the tangled branches, I search for my way,
But every few steps, I stumble and splay,
The breeze tells me secrets, oh what do they mean?
I'll have to ask grass, it's surely a keen.

A deer makes a pun, and I snort with delight,
While the raccoons gather for a comedy night,
Caught in the moment, like vines I will twine,
In this goofy green world, everything's fine.

With every leaf rustle, there's humor to share,
Even nature's mishaps are met with good care,
So here in the branches where echoes grow bold,
Laughter's a currency more treasured than gold.

In the Company of Wings

In the company of wings, I dare to explore,
With flaps and with flutters, excitement galore,
A bluebird squawks jokes from a high leafy place,
While I scramble up boughs, trying to keep pace.

A dizzying dance on a branch that's too thin,
Mocked by the robins as they cheer, "Let's begin!"
I stumble and fumble, but laughter stays near,
Through branches so twisted, oh what a grand cheer!

With owls telling tales in their wise, sleepy tone,
I trip on a root, landing quite near a stone,
"Watch where you step!" the wise old owl hoots,
While I wave at the thrush in my funny green suit.

A parade of the quirky, wings flutter so bright,
As feathers and giggles fill up the cool night,
In this winged company, my heart starts to sing,
For the nature of laughter loans joy on a spring.

www.ingramcontent.com/pod-product-compliance
Lightning Source LLC
Chambersburg PA
CBHW072142200426
43209CB00051B/277